The BBQ Restaurant Survival Guide

By

Mark Groce

Valerie Groce

copyright © 2016

Table of Contents

Our Story

Our Transition from Mobile to Restaurant

Question: HOW DO YOU WANT TO START?

The Health Department

Health Department Isn't So Scary

Food Service Permit and the Application for Them

Food Safety

Sample Drawing of Mobile Setup

List of Items Needed For Mobile Setup

Finding the Perfect Mobile Location

Opportunities Abound!

Finding Your Retail Space!

The Restaurant Space and the Lease

How Much Should You Pay for Rent?

The Legal Stuff...and a word of warning

Mobile Smoker Selection

Indoor (Commercial) Smokers

Your Choice of Wood is Critical

BBQ Restaurant Kitchen and Hood Systems – Do I need it?

Our Secrets to Consistently Good BBQ in a High Production Environment

Why Change a Thing?

Mobile Method vs. Smoker Oven Method

Restaurant Equipment Explained

Minimum Supplies Needed for Kitchen

The BBQ Process for High Volume Sales

Pulled Pork (Boston Butts)

What To Do With Product Leftover

The Vacuum Sealer – Best Invention Ever!

Ribs

Two Options to Reheat Ribs

Brisket

Chicken

Corned Beef (don't knock it until you try it)

The All Important Side Dishes

Do Not Prepare Too Much Ahead

My Daily Routine

Kitchen and Restaurant Layout

Plates and Forks (fancy) or Plastic (hillbilly..)

Seating

Food Distributors and Sourcing Product

Getting Stuff for Free!

The Importance of Wood Suppliers

Advertising

Online Promotions and Coupons – A Risky Distraction

Groupon and Similar Programs

Loyalty Programs

Radio?

Shared Revenue Plans

News Paper Advertising During The Holidays

Social Media (whichever is popular these days)

Local Businesses and Hotels

The Dreaded Internet Review Sites

Catering is Big Business

Equipment Needed for Catering

Transporting Food

Quoting and Preparing The Right Amount

Holiday Catering and Party Orders

Food Cost Considerations

Management and POS Systems Explained

Taking Credit Cards

The Not So Glamorous - Cleaning

What to Expect Opening Day

Staffing

Payroll and Other Stuff

Final Thoughts

Our Story

I was in the IT industry for well over 20 years, and my wife was a Corporate and IT Trainer and Process Management professional for 15 years. As a consultant, I traveled pretty extensively as a Certified Trainer teaching advanced networking techniques to other engineers. In the end I took a job as a Senior Systems Engineer for a good sized company (no more travel). Then one day in 2008 I found myself out of a job. *Sound familiar?* It happened before, but usually I landed another in less than a month. No worries...

A year later I still had no job and nothing on the horizon. Fortunately my wife had a good job with benefits. What other skills do I possess that can earn? Well, I had been making BBQ almost as long as being an IT guy. So, I was kicking around the idea of taking my love of BBQ which was just a passionate hobby and try selling it on the street a few days a week.

I thought I just needed a mobile smoker, tables and stuff (I did not realize where this would end up at the time). My wonderful wife was enthusiastic about it and thought it was a great idea (*I think she just wanted me out of the house*), so we scraped up the money for a smoker and miscellaneous items (tables, pop-up tent, etc), and found a great little smoker on Craigslist. It was a drum style made from an old propane tank on a single axle with good tires, built well and the price was right at 1800.00. It was in Missouri, 16 hours round trip. We got it back home and I could not have been happier. Still had know Idea what I was doing, but excited!

The Bad News

Everything was looking great until the bad news hit. A few days after we got back my wife was laid off. Now it's time to worry. It was sink or swim time and I could not have had a better partner in the pool with me, my wife. No, neither of us knew what we were doing!

As I stated earlier, we had little money to risk and little choice other than to start somewhere like a parking lot. I figured this would also give us a chance to gauge "market interest" in our product. We found a good location only three blocks from our house. The next task was to talk to the owner of the lot and get permission.

It was once a gas station built sometime in the early 60's, but had not been a functioning station in many years however and was kept in wonderful shape. White tiles covering the outside walls, with a 1940's glass globe gas pump on display between the two garage doors and flawless black top parking lot that was smooth as glass. It was currently being used by a gentleman named Vic to store a few of his classic cars and some odds-and-ends. It was his little getaway and his show piece during the summer festivals in this historic small town in Ohio.

When I first spoke to him about using the front lot to sell BBQ he was somewhat reluctant but gave me his number so we could discuss it further when he was not so busy. I followed up in a few days after he had time to think about it, and even offered him a percentage of my sales. In the end he agreed to let us use the lot so long as we kept it clean. He also declined my offer to take a percentage and wished us luck! He signed a brief letter giving us permission and that was it.

We are going into the BBQ Business!

I slept very little. I was just too excited and a little scared. I only ever made BBQ for friends...in my backyard. I guess this was not much different...

My plan was to have the smoker fired up no later than 11pm, meat on by midnight. Damn if I did not have that thing blazing by 9pm. My problem however was I didn't know how much to make. Would 100lbs be too much? Probably... So I decided our best course of action would be to start small, really small. Hopefully sell out and just make more the next day. The wife agreed. We decided on 20lbs of Pork Butt (2 roast), and 20lbs of chicken leg quarters. I thought this was too little, but relented to her better judgment.

I was meticulous on maintaining the smoker temp at a perfect 225-230 degrees all night. My wife took care of all the sides in the morning. At 10:30am, we started to pack everything into the Jeep, hooked up the smoker (still smoking), and drove the three blocks. We started unpacking and were set up by 10:40 AM and ready to go by 11am. We served from 11am until 2pm. In addition to the 20lbs of Pork and 20lbs of Chicken we had coleslaw in a cooler and assorted chips (1oz bags) and soft drinks. We sold out by 1:30 and did just over $200 in sales!

Of course, after expenses and food cost, we only made about $130, but you have to start somewhere!

Over the next two weeks we changed very little in what we offered, selling out most days. By the 3rd week we added other items such as brisket or ribs on some days, and tried out some other sides as well. We made more as our customers and sales increased.

As our exposure grew and more people talked about us we had people offering us more opportunities, from leads on festivals, new locations, and catering gigs. I remember the 3rd time we posted on Facebook that we had ribs for lunch, the city employees met us at the lot at 10:30 and helped us set up so they could have first option on the ribs before we sold out. It was that time that we really knew we had something going on.

Then there was "Crazy Bob"

Bob is the owner of a local "entertainment farm". It's like a giant produce stand with live entertainment on the weekends, pick-your-own berries, cider, and stuff for kids. Anyway, he asked if we would be willing to come to his place on weekends and serve his customers!

So we did the parking lot "lunch thing" Monday through Friday, and the "farm thing" as we called it Saturday and Sunday. 7 Days a week for the next 2 months. By this time we had help, as our son Devoreaux and his best friend Chad were out of School. They were great help on the weekends as we got VERY busy!

By Autumn, Valerie started complaining about the cold weather and we were making enough and had enough customers to look at a more permanent location which I will discuss in a moment, but our last day in a parking lot was pretty insane. It was a Friday. We served 196 people in 3 hours. I think we need to find someplace...inside...and fast.

This was our beginning. Now let's get to yours...

Our Transition from Mobile to Restaurant

My ultimate goal was to eventually open a restaurant, but the decision to start mobile was made for us due to our non-existent cash flow. This was only a temporary start, as we were operating with Temporary Food Service Permits which limited us to just (10) 7 day permits per calendar year (discussed in detail in the Health and Building section). We would either have to invest in a "permanent mobile" setup (same setup used by State Fair type vendors), or open a restaurant.

Fortunately I had already known of a location that met most of my criteria:

Was once a restaurant (should be cheap to get reopened!)

Located in a busy strip mall on a the same road we started

Was just a few blocks away (so our customers can find us)

The anchor store is a Shell Station with lots of traffic

A spot for the smoker

A motivated building owner

As stated, it had been a number of restaurants before…all failed. Some were due to family disputes, others to bad food concepts (Fish Taco's... in Ohio?). The only commonality I heard about these failures was the location itself being a poor choice due to being away from the other food concepts down the road.

This may be true but I had no other choice at the time and due to a motivated owner, we were risking very little, it was the only vacant location in town, and time was limited. I only had 2 more weeks of permits available. I felt it was worth a try. Our first full year gross sales were $369,000, second year was $421,000. In a town of 22,000 people, I would say our location was pretty darn good.

The Building Itself was nothing unusual. In fact, it was quite boring. It was a typical strip mall with red brick fascia on the top half, with a concrete colored stone work on the bottom running the length of the building. t was about 1400 sq ft inside with 2 bathrooms down the hallway to the back left and a dining room in the front half, and kitchen in the back.

The kitchen was 600 sq ft, huge for a restaurant this size. There was no office space and very little storage. It had been stripped of everything except the Hood/Ansul system. No sink, or anything else. This was going to be work getting the place ready for business.

I negotiated the lease (see "Negotiating the Lease"), got it reviewed by an attorney (*never sign without someone having a look*) and moved my operation from the parking lot at the old station to the parking lot in front of the new "future" restaurant.

Over the next few weeks we worked on getting open. As we made money under the tent, we put our proceeds into purchasing equipment. First I bought a sink, had the sink installed and then we bought a commercial fridge. After that, a few stainless tables, etc. We got our health inspection within 3 weeks of signing the lease. We passed and were allowed to open!

The dining room was great! We had borrowed card tables and folding steel chairs all with matching vinyl table cloths in the name of continuity. Well, the only thing in continuity actually. We called it quaint... We hand wrote all the tickets, and it was cash only, but by golly – we were open! We had no idea what I was doing then, but somehow we managed it.

Things Learned...that this book would have helped me on?

- <u>Correct</u> kitchen equipment
- <u>Correct</u> smoker *(size and design)*
- Efficient kitchen design based on task and yes, having the right equipment to start with
- Had inspected the electrical service/capacity BEFORE signing the lease *(could have (gotten the building owner to have helped with the cost)*
- Accepting credit cards from the beginning and how that's done *(lost a lot of corporate catering in the beginning)*
- Portion control!!!
- Cost controls *(P&L's were not that scary after all)*
- How to deal with all the vendors, people wanting "donations", and endless interruptions
- Advertising
- Hiring, payroll, and letting people go *(I hated that part)*
- Not having to work 20 hours per day

And SO much more…

Question: HOW DO YOU WANT TO START?

Like everything else it comes down to money and time. More of one and less of the other can decide that pretty quickly. Otherwise it just depends on your resources, family situation, and opportunities available to you at the moment. Less money and lots of time you may start as I did, if you have the money, and have found a great location that will save you time when you are ready.

Either way this book can help.

If you're flying by the seat of your pants like I did, I highly recommend a second income in your household. We lived in poverty at first, and while we found it a character building experience for the entire family, I wouldn't recommend it if you can avoid it. I remember when my wife rejoined the corporate world; our son exclaimed *"does this mean we aren't poor anymore?"* I was very grateful for my wife's income as I learned about the peaks and valleys of seasonal sales.

So, we will start with my situation, little money, and lots of time and want to build your customer base first and determine if there is a market for your wonderful BBQ. If you are looking to go straight into opening BBQ restaurant then skip this section.

Either way you may want to review the section on **Smokers**. *Having one that works well for doing outside (lot) sales may or may not work well in a restaurant setting. Having the right equipment from the start will do you well and save many hours for other things like sleeping, not to mention money.*

Dining Area

There are a few things that make a good design from a bad one. Efficient flow, and keeping the quality of product should be your first consideration when planning your design. Though you may not have a lot of choice in the matter depending on the space you find however. Most spaces were designed for another restaurant and planned flow. Paying for a complete remodel to fit your particular needs may not be feasible either.

First we have to decide on what type of restaurant you want to have?

> Full Service (Wait Staff)
>
> Fast Casual (customer orders at counter and run it out)
>
> Buffet style (plan on going broke)
>
> Cafeteria (think Chipotle)
>
> Hybrid of these?

In our first restaurant, the customer came up and ordered and we ran the food out. Based on the design of the space this made the most sense for a number of reasons,

> We did not have the space for Server Stations for the wait staff
>
> The food was put together so quickly that having server staff would have just slowed things down.

Our customers were always amazed at the speed they got served.
My response was "9 Hours to make it, 90 seconds to get it"!

Plates and Forks (fancy) or Plastic (hillbilly..)

We chose plastic. Plastic boats lined with foil sheets we bought at GFS, and heavy weight forks, spoons and knives (fancy hillbilly).

> We did not have room for a dishwasher in our kitchen and the chemicals are expensive
>
> The labor involved
>
> Breakage can add up

The down side of going hillbilly

> If you go full service with nice dishes and wait staff you can go higher on your menu pricing (5-10%) and increase profitability.

> Customers will throw the plastic boats away and paying for plastic ware all the time can add up too

Our customer base and location would not have allowed us to demand menu pricing enough to justify the added cost of a full service restaurant, so we kept it simple. But if you have the right restaurant location and have the added value of full service by all means that's the direction you should go.

Seating

Proper layout of the restaurant and arrangement of seating, and seating capacity can depend on the number of seats you have and or need, and the space available. Too much seating your restaurant looks empty, too little and you can lose money on walkouts. Proper design based on the various situations and options requires far more depth and well beyond the scope of this book. There are many books and resources on the internet that specialize in just this topic, including software (not needed in most cases).

Food Distributors and Sourcing Product

There are large food distributors everywhere. Sysco, Gordon Food Service (GFS), and US Foods are all national (and international) providers of food to restaurants. They are pretty competitive in pricing but not all of them can or will have the exact items you need. If you have a sadistic nature, you can put them up against each other for the smallest things and see if they take the bait.

They will ask you for either a list of the items you use or a copy of your menu (or both) and come up with a list with pricing (shopping list) from which you make your orders.

All the big guys have a minimum order amount (money or count of items/boxes) before they will make a delivery. In the beginning we did not have a big enough order to get deliver so we found another option. We also found that there was no discounts with delivery service, and often the prices were higher than going to the stores ourselves.

GFS (Gordon Food Service)

These stores supply restaurants and the public alike, with no membership required. We signed up for a commercial account with them. We went in daily and shopped for the items we needed, or they special ordered something for us if not on the shelf already. It was great for cash-flowing but pricing wasn't the best. The great thing about this was the rebate. A 7% rebate on all the purchases for the year. Our first rebate check was over $7000!

> We bought a car...

They also had delivery service to the restaurant, but the prices were higher and the rebate program didn't apply. That was enough to get one of us in the car.

Smaller Regional Distributors

These typically do not have the same minimum order requirements as the big guys. They target the specialty restaurants and smaller establishments. They are competitive with pricing and have far better customer service. It's not unusual to put in an emergency order and the sales guy would show up in an hour. I don't have a list of the vendors for you as they are local/regional. Don't be surprised if they show up even before you open!

They are like Meat Ninja's…sneaky fast…and they don't give up, so keep a few in your pocket!

What I did find was these smaller vendors could get me great deals with meat or produce, but the other items I used daily weren't as competitive. It's just like any other store as a civilian, where you get a discount here, but pay through the teeth in another aisle. For the long haul, we found meats were our best bet for challenging them to get competitive.

Your Local Grocery

Don't overlook your local options either. One of the local (independent) grocery stores allowed us to buy brisket through them with their discount, only charging us a few cents more per pound and they priced them out individually for purchase. Also, if they got a hot opportunity for pork butts that reached their freeze-by date, they would buy them all up for us and keep them in the freezer until we wanted them. The great part of this was the space it saved in our coolers and not having to buy an entire case at once (better cash flow). They let us buy just what we needed when we needed it. I would just walk back to the cooler each day and grab what I needed. The benefit for them was I would buy plenty of other items we needed while I was there. Many of these items were less expensive there than the "restaurant supply" stores.

These restaurant suppliers are selling you large quantities, but you don't always get a discount for buying in bulk, so if you're trying to keep things as frugal as you can, it pays to compare prices, and so what if you're opening 5 boxes of macaroni instead of one bag?

Note on Sourcing Product

The Health Department will want a chain-of-custody as well. On the food service application they will ask you where you are getting the food you prepare. You need to be able to show where you purchased your food in case something should happen. So, you can't dress and smoke that deer you shot!

Getting Stuff for Free!

It's great owning a restaurant. Everyone wants you to serve their stuff.
You will be given all kinds of samples (sometimes cases) of stuff to try.

You can even ask for kitchen equipment. The war between Coke and Pepsi is to your advantage! Regardless of which one you decided to go with tell them you want a Single Glass Door Cooler. Hell, make it two. One to sell canned or bottled soda, one for you to use in your kitchen (be honest...) and the fountain system too! Don't pay a dime for install! I want the first round of syrup for free too! I got all this for both restaurants without too much hassle. They pushed back a little but I just tell them "Pepsi said they would do it....but I like Coke more and really want you guys". It's true...

The Importance of Wood Suppliers

As discussed earlier its vital you locate a good supply of wood as soon as possible whether you start in a parking lot or a restaurant. You will go through a lot of it and use this to your advantage. The more you buy the better the price. But, you must watch the quality of wood you get. Ask for a small delivery (or a few logs if picking up) which to test. Let them know what you are using it for (not a fireplace). So it must be of sufficient size to fit in your firebox. Let them know its critical that it be consistent. If not you will go somewhere else.

You can test the moisture content by dropping it a few feet onto concrete. If it makes a solid thud and is really heavy it's too wet. Sounds "clinky" and is really lightweight its too dry. You want to hear a "clunk". You will pick this up pretty quickly once you have burned (literally) through as much as I have.

You will get plenty of people coming in to your restaurant wanting to sell wood "at a bargain". I pass. I've been there and done that. They usually run out of supply quickly and I'm left hanging. A good supplier counts on my order as much as I count on him and I won't risk it.

Advertising

Just know right now that there is no "magic bullet" when it comes to advertising. So, mix it up. Here are a few of the things we did and the results we got. Just know that this ALL DEPENDS ON YOUR MARKET. What may or may not work for me may work for you just fine. That's why you want to try different things. There are many other resources that focus on this important topic, so I will leave it to the "experts" for the details. I will however let you in on what we did and the results.

Online Promotions and Coupons – A Risky Distraction

Unless you are a pizza restaurant do not get in the habit of using coupons. I almost expect a coupon to be available for a pizza, because who pays full price? But considering the food cost for a BBQ joint (much higher than pizza) it's not a good position to be in with customers becoming used to a discount price.

The only exception where we offered coupons was for local fund raising promotions. The football team had a discount card with our offer stated on it with other local companies, and another school had those Entertainment Books that my wife hates (another story I'll not go into). I'm sure there were one or two others, but you get the idea. Our offer was a small one, but it got peoples attention that we were here. The thing that makes fund raising coupons different than the other coupon sources is that (1) they are helping the local communities, getting us in the good graces with the families in town, and (2) they take care of all the printing costs, distribution, etc. We pay nothing more than honoring the coupons when they come into our place.

Groupon and Similar Programs

We used this service just after opening our first location and happy with what we intended it to do, which was let people in surrounding areas know who we were.

The way it works is you pick the level of promotion value. The promotion, $30 for $15 for example would mean the customers pays $15 and gets $30 worth of purchasing value in the form of a printed (or mobile device) coupon. Of that $15 you, the restaurant, get 50% ($7.50) of each "groupon" sold. When doing this you need to consider your food and labor cost (Prime Cost) and a little profit if possible when determining the promotion you wish to offer.

The most valuable component of Groupon is their ability to target a geographical area and type of customer (your target customer) that receives the promotion.

When customers register with Groupon they provide consumer information to include there name and address, and the products and or services they wish to receive discounts for. This allows Groupon to "target" the offer to specific customers in your area. Our goal was to get people to know who, and where we were. Groupon limited the offer to 3 zip codes (ours, and North/South of us). Well, 986 "Groupons" sold in two days, and got the word out that we were in business!

The Down Side to These Programs?

- Be prepared for a stampede of people with coupons in hand the first week. Your gross sales will look great but your cash drawer will be light.

- The "Groupons" are valid for a year and on the last two weeks, expect a stampede similar to what you had the first week, along with the matching light drawer.

- If your business is lean in the winter months this could cause cash flow problems.

- The purchase value ($15) never expires (Federal Consumer Law), so years later, they can come in and use this Groupon for it's original purchased price.

- Your portion of the sale (50%) is paid out over months but your cost is immediate as the Groupons come rolling in.

Loyalty Programs

Loyalty programs, done correctly, are a great way of generating new business, as increased customer retention.

Punch Cards (our favorite)

These were a great success. We had "*Porkaholic Punch Cards*" - business cards made that had 10 pig butts printed on the back. Every time they came in we punched it. A customer by the name of Marvin went through 26 cards in 8 months and held the record! Rewarding customers for their business is a great way to retain them, and to promote the business.

Other Options...not for us.

I know there are many Loyalty Program options available but I preferred to stay with the punch cards for a number of important reasons, as opposed to the new electronic "services" being shopped around by various companies. Rather than explain it, you can see one here https://getbelly.com/ First, I must admit that I am a little biased on this. As I was in the Technology Industry for over 20 years, and liked playing with fire and meat everyday, the last thing I wanted in my restaurant was anything reminding me of it!

That aside, I had other more practical reasons to not use them:

- Something computerized can and will break

- I did not want a piece of technology acting as an intermediary between me and my customer. Technology has its place, but I want to look my customer in the eye as I punch his card, telling him "You're half way to a free meal Marvin!"

- These plans cost money to participate

- The time required to manage it

- Some people may be turned off by the fact that someone is tracking their moves. Just ask them how they feel about their local grocery stores discount cards.

What about Radio?

Radio advertising can be used effectively to get your brand out but it must be done consistently over a long period to really get the reach you want. The companies that use radio where you live and recognize, advertise on radio for years to get that level of recognition. Fancy jingles, and repeating the number 50 times in 30 seconds. Regardless, I never really thought it was a valid option without a really good discount being offered. My customer base was only a 10 mile radius of me, and thought radio was not focused enough for the money it cost.

There is a good chance to get free radio plug! Offer to bring them lunch! I called and asked what time I could drop off lunch for the staff. They were broadcasting 6 stations from one building and ALL the radio people from the other stations grabbed a bit during commercials. I was mentioned on at least three different stations!

Food is cheaper than cash. From there, expect the advertising sales exec's will be calling to get your business. It doesn't hurt to hear the offer as their promotions change throughout the year.

Shared Revenue Plans

Many local stations offer "Shared Revenue Plans" as an advertising option. Think of it as Radio mixed with Groupon. The plans are similar to Groupon, but they offer On Air promotion and on their website to promote your restaurant and the offer. In addition to the portion of the revenue you get (same as Groupon) they will also give you a limited number of real (not affiliated with the promotion) radio commercial spots for you to advertise your restaurant directly. They typically get you paid faster, and you get airtime not just at night when no one is listening but at peak times as well.

To determine if this program is really a value, and you really feel Radio will benefit you, ask them for a copy of their current ad rates first. It's not unusual for them to promote the program when there is a lot of available (unsold) airtime time that you could buy at a discount without having to commit to a revenue split.

News Paper Advertising During The Holidays

Unless it is a local/regional paper that is read heavily in your market by your customers I would avoid it. Yes, ad cost is a bargain compared to a few years ago, but that's because a lot fewer people are reading their news in print. That being said, we did get a good response from a smoked turkey promotion for Thanksgiving from our local community free paper for a low cost, but it was the only time we advertised in the paper.

Social Media (whichever is popular these days)

This was our most successful and dynamic marketing tool in my opinion.
Our tool of choice was **Facebook**. We started from our days underneath a tent posting where we would be popping up through the week and on the weekend.

We got a couple hundred followers during that period. When we moved under a roof, we started posting about our specials, and what kind of soup we had that day. Think about it – hundreds of smartphones with this feeding right in as they're getting hungry for lunch or dinner. It was perfect and we could change it at our own whims. For a small amount of money (only $5-$10), I could even push my postings out to my fans with their friends. I got great joy seeing how a message started at our fan base, and spread throughout the area, from person to person as they shared the post on their pages for others to see.

It was also an open forum for us to communicate with our customers.

They could answer back, ask questions, make comments, etc. Many posted about their good experiences and some posted if they had a bad one. I loved it because we could publicly show our concern and make remedy of the situation in front of everyone.

Local Businesses and Hotels

Make a similar offer of bringing food in to the staff to introduce yourself. Hotels will send guests your way and you want to target businesses that will either refer you or order catering in the future.

Promotion Days

Give a discount, or free drink on certain days. Especially with slow days at the beginning of the week.

We had:

- Mustache Monday *(real, fake, draw on, but no finger staches)*

- Two Punch Tuesday *(with the Porkaholics Punch Card)*

- Workbadge Wednesday

- Sundays were $5 off family meal

The Dreaded Internet Review Sites

For the most part *Urbanspoon.com, Yelp.com, Tripadvisor.com, Etc.* should not be counted on for dependable consumer information. Having good Customer Reviews is great (our average score was 4-4.5 out of 5), but I find that for the most part to be a distraction more than anything.

Many "reviews" come from those I like to call "Serial Reviewers". They have written "suggestions" (*complaints*) for every restaurant they've gone to (*most site will show you their history*). It gives them some sense of self importance and thinks it's there "civic duty" to protect the community! Some were internet trolls before it was a thing.

You must not depend on these reviews as a tool of improvement. One person will hate the green beans, and a few comments later another will rave about them. If you can please 80% of the people you are doing great!

There is one benefit to these sites, and that's looking for patterns. If you have a number of reviews mentioning a similar item or problem investigate it immediately.

The most important thing and I cannot stress this enough;

DO NOT REPLY TO ANY COMMENT!

DO NOT ARGUE OR CONTRADICT ANYTHING!

EVEN IF YOU KNOW THEY'RE WRONG!

These sites are for customers, not you, the restaurant to interact. It is acceptable to acknowledge a "problem" and that it has or will be handled but that's it. No apologies, or "give us another chance", nothing.

Yes you want this kind of information brought to your attention, preferably in the restaurant and in private, but some customers feel better doing it anonymously. If you confront them in "public", others will take offense and then you have a much bigger problem.

Segway to a small rant we couldn't find the right place to fit elsewhere:

It's the customers that don't review that you should be concerned about. Pay attention to those dining with you. If you spend time watching and talking with your customers in the dining room you will learn a lot more than any "review" site could ever tell you!

What are your customers leaving behind and not eating? Do they not like it? Go to the kitchen and give it a taste (not from the plate, but from the stuff your serving..ick). If it is good (to you) maybe it's just not to their liking, and offer them something else! It shows you are paying attention and care. This will allow you to fix something before it's a problem, and or making a customer know that you care enough to ask.

Catering is Big Business

Catering is one of the most profitable aspects of a BBQ restaurant. In our restaurant we received anywhere from 20-30 calls a month (more during holidays) asking for catering information and quotes, for small parties to events of 1000 people or more. With the processes we have already covered in this book you will find that just a couple of people can mange to produce vast amounts of great BBQ and the good news is that they will ask where this fabulous food came from. That generates even more business for you and or your restaurant!

How much business can one restaurant handle with these processes?

In one day, we catered an event for a VERY large international company for 1200+ people as well as serving hundreds more in our restaurant during the busiest festival day of the year. Sales totaled more than $9000 in a single day, and we got follow up catering orders from employees and festival attendees for months after.

> *A word of warning: Don't hesitate to turn down an event. If you are not confident in getting it done! Be it the staff's ability, or just your comfort level. The restaurant comes first. If you are to busy, apologize and tell them no. If you get overwhelmed, both the gig and the restaurant will suffer and you will not come out looking good either way.*

Equipment Needed for Catering

When we say catering, what we are really talking about is the transporting of food regardless of any additional services (setup, serving, cleanup, etc) you wish to provide. So for now, it's all about the food and the gear you need to get it done.

Catering equipment in general is pretty specific to the industry whether its BBQ or Brazed Pork Medallions with Seared Potatoes its all the same. We will discuss what each piece is and the best way to use it for BBQ.

When dealing with the public and keeping with food safety standards we are required to use specialized "approved" items and materials. This means NSF certification.

All food carriers must have an NSF approved designation which says it has met or exceeded NSF requirements for food Safety, and must have an NSF label, or stamp demonstrating it. You will usually see this on the inside door, a panel, or other obvious place.

The only possible exception is for cold items such as Coleslaw or similar food stuffs that can be in individually portioned (foam container with lid) servings. I was allowed to keep these in a non-NSF certified cooler with ice, but the key here is that they were portioned already and ready for immediate serving. This does not mean your particular inspector would be as forgiving.

So that cooler you bought from Walmart for the fishing trip last summer probably isn't NSF certified and cannot be used for carrying pulled pork in it. So, be sure to look for the NSF symbol.

Transporting Food

Cambro Insulated Cabinets

There are a number of manufactures of similar products, but I personally like Cambro's. They come in a variety of sizes and models to suit every type of situation. Though they can be quite expensive they are well worth it. They are designed to stack one atop another which is very helpful at events when space is limited. You can review Cambro's catering equipment here http://www.cambro.com/Catering/

These are the models I prefer do to the size and versatility
(I used one once instead of a cooler to hold soft drinks. I just turned it lid up and took up far less deck space).

They also make a number of accessories for these units such as Insulated Partitions that separate the Hot Food, from the Cold Food in the same carrier. Very handy indeed!.

Cambro Camcarrier

I like these due to their size. They hold about 6 full size hotel pans. The built in handles make transport a little easier, but they are also used to interlock another unit when placed on top.

> **Tip # 5**
>
> If not filled to capacity with hot food, it will have trouble keeping food warm due to the volume of unused space absorbing the available heat. To counteract this I just provide a supplemental heat source.
>
> You need one full size hotel pan and 2-3 Ziplock or other food storage containers with sealable lids.
>
> Fill each container with water and microwave until very hot but not boiling. Place these in the full size hotel pan. Place the pan in the bottom of the carrier and load it up with food!

I've had these stay hot for 8 hours even when the door was being opened to remove items for serving.

Cambro Ultra Pan Carrier

These are larger units. They can hold almost twice as much as the Camcarriers. But due to their size you WILL need help moving them to and from a site. They are "stackable" as well but I recommend you get the available cart with caster if you plan to do so.

Of course you can purchase these used or at auction but you should inspect them first. They are very rugged but the latch kits or seals if broken can be expensive to replace.

Other Items

Once you transport the food and lets assume you are also doing the setup and service, there are a few other items you will need. They are by no means expensive or fancy because this is BBQ, and we're not fancy.

Wire Chaffing Rack

Ones like these that stand straighter (without a taper to them) as you will be setting up a double-boiler type system.

It's ironic that one of the biggest problems with keeping food hot is not burning it! Chafing fuel creates hot spots with dense food such as pulled pork. To remedy this we use a double-boiler system.

One 4" Deep Full Sized Foil Pan (or 4" Stainless Hotel Pan) and Two 2" Half Sized Foil Pans of product.

Fill the full sized pan with ½ inch of water and place in the chaffer. Light Chafing Fuel and place in rack. Then place each Half Foil Pan with meat or sides into the pan. Keep an eye on the water level as you replace with pans when empty.

Other Items needed for catering:

- Folding Tables (most times they are customer provided but verify. You can also charge for transport and use.)
- Stainless Tongs (set for each tray of meat actively being served)
- Stainless Slotted Serving Spoons (set for each side)
- Latex Gloves
- Hand Sanitizer
- Plenty of Towels for Cleanup as needed
- Plenty of BBQ Sauce!

Other Items that may be needed are:

(These I charge extra for so the customer may decide to purchase themselves)

- Plastic ware
- Napkins
- Buns
- Drinks

Setup

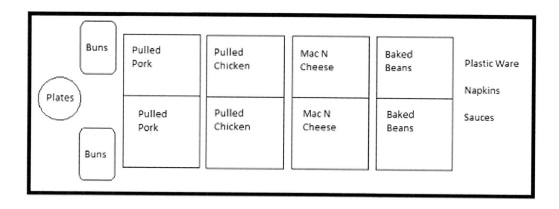

For larger events you will want a "mirror setup". This just means setting up 2 lines allowing for quicker food service.

You will want to place beverages away from the food table. This will force traffic away from the line increasing flow.

Quoting and Preparing The Right Amount

The first thing I ask is the number and type of guests. Men eat more than women, and kids 12 and under eat about the same or more than older guests.

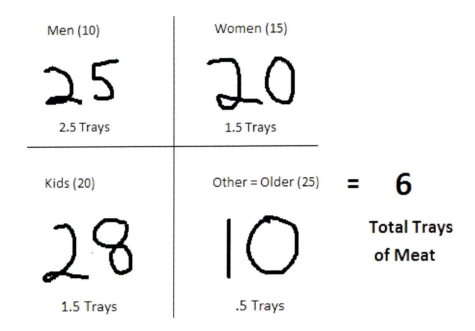

I draw this out on a piece of paper and fill in the numbers as I get them:
I already know that the average serving for a group of men is 10-12 people per 5lb tray of pork. So if the number is 15 that's 1.5 trays, and so on.

Round up on the amount if necessary as you don't want to come up short, but let the customer know this as they may not like having food leftover that they cannot use. Otherwise, let them make the decision. This works with all meats, but sides are a little different. If you order that many sides (enough of each for everyone to have everything) you will have over sold by a huge amount. Get the customers opinion here.

Explain that the Mac-n-Cheese is very popular so get 6 trays, enough for everyone (in the above example). But I would only recommend 4 trays of Baked Beans, and 3 trays of Green Beans and Coleslaw. The more sides they order the more you will have leftover! I try to limit sides to no more than 3 If possible to avoid this.

Another great tip for good customer service is to provide a list of recipe ideas of what they might do with some of those leftovers.

Deposits

For larger events and those wanting us to do the serving, I always take a deposit of 50% to reserve the date and time. This was helpful in our earlier days when we may not have had the cash flow to buy the supplies needed. Smaller parties (less than 50), I didn't require it.

When Quoting Food

I had plenty of customers that just wanted pork. For smaller events and they know what their guest will eat this is fine, but for larger parties you must consider the implications of this as not everyone eats pulled pork! Primarily for religious or dietary reason, but I've seen a lot of kids that don't do pork either.

So you may want to offer Pulled Chicken as an option, or better yet Split Leg Quarters. The profit margin is great as you can buy 10 lbs for $5, and sell it all day for $25, and the labor cost and time to produce it is significantly less than anything else. I price it a lot cheaper than Pulled Chicken or Pulled Pork to encourage them to buy it. The kids also love the drumsticks "meat on a stick". Don't fall for the vegetarian request. Your specialty is meat, and you don't want to be known for black bean burgers, do you? It's not just snobbery, but these one-off's really put a wrench in your workflow back in the kitchen, and remember, those in the kitchen are also serving people in-house. It's important to keep their workflow smooth.

Charging for Other Items

In my perfect world, a catering order would be the customer coming in and picking up everything at an agreed upon time. Much of the time, they wanted me to do more than that, which required adding more staff to accommodate these extra services. I charged for most everything to compensate for it. Delivery was $20 within 10 miles, and .50 a mile thereafter. Setup was $15 dollars if table is provided, and $10 for the use of my tables plus the setup fee. Labor was $20 per hour per staff member. Cleanup was $25 plus the hourly rate already mentioned (we provided the trash collection containers and the liners for this fee).

At first we bid what we thought were high numbers for this stuff because we didn't want to get involved that deeply, but darn it if the customers didn't just nod and agree to whatever we quoted so they could just sit back and enjoy their party. If you want to be competitive on your pricing and each market is different so you may just call around to your "competitors" and get a quote on everything I just mentioned. This will give you a good start as to where you should be. Just don't forget to factor in time and labor costs when making these quotes.

Holiday Catering and Carry Out Party Orders

The holidays can be very profitable for a BBQ restaurant. Promoting your offerings is important, however to making the most of the short holiday season before leading into the winter months when business for all restaurants is at its lowest. So I will cover what items sell the best for the big three (Thanksgiving, Christmas, and New Years). The promotion method however will be the same regardless.

Turkeys

These are a gold mine. I ordered them in quantity from the local grocery store. As all the retailers are ordering from the same distributors (unless you want free-range birds) it really does not matter which store, so shop by who will give you the best "quantity" price. One year I was getting them for .72 cents per pound. I spoke to the meat manager at Walmart one year and they reserved the turkeys for us for the week of Thanksgiving so we could purchase each day what we needed of fresh product at the weights we specified.

Turkey pricing was straight forward. Large turkeys (18-20lbs +) were $60, and small ones (10-12lbs) were $45. Profit was great at $45 for the large, and $35 for the small. When you get 100+ birds sold in a few days it adds up quick. On average we did $5000 on just the turkeys, not to mention everything else.

Smoking Turkeys

If you are a BBQ hobbyist I'm sure you have done your share of birds, but getting that many done on time is tenuous at best. When people have a party they want there stuff on time! But, if you do not feel confident in providing a good product on time do not even offer it. There are many other less challenging options. Nothing worse than someone bringing back an under-cooked bird and looking to you to fix it!

Staggered Approach

Depending on the number of birds and the size of your smoker will determine how many you can get done in one smoking cycle so its best to group them by size, smalls then large.

Once thawed you can smoke them until an internal temp of 175-180F is reached. As they reach temperature, pull them from the smoker and wrap in plastic wrap, then place in Foil Roasting pan. Place pan in the Cres Cor. The Cres Cor can hold approximately 20 small birds and 12-14 large birds. If this is full and you have room on the smoker you will add one additional layer of Aluminum foil and place back on the smoker.

Test Runs

I would do a few test birds before you do anything. 2 Large and 2 small will do fine. You need to carefully track how long it takes you to THAW (if from frozen) AND SMOKE time to reach proper temp. This will tell you what time you need to get the real process started.

Thawing Problem

If you have mass birds to get done thawing space can be a bigger problem than smoker space. If you do not have a walk in cooler to slack (thaw) them just ask the place you will purchase them from to move them into there cooler 2-5 days before you need them. If they have to stack them in cases they will need even more time as it could take a week to thaw. Ask them for a best guess. It's there cooler and I hope they would know!

Hams

These are the easiest of holiday items to prepare (and our favorite to eat). The best seller was the spiral cut hams, and was the only one we offered. You could do it by the pound but, like the turkeys, we did Large (10+lbs) and Small (5-6lbs). We charged $50 and $35 respectively, The profit was not as high but MUCH easier to prep and get out the door.

Preparation for Ham:

Rub it down with yellow mustard until completely covered. You will not taste it as it will dissipate during the smoking process, but it is used as "glue" to hold the dry rub you put on it next.

You can use your favorite rub, but adding a pungent spice (rosemary, clove, tyme, celery seed, or even basil) along with more than usual brown sugar. You will want to "cake" this on the outside completely covering the mustard until no more rub will stick. Do not RUB it in, it will just make a mess.

Place on the smoker for 4-5 hours or until a temp of 145-150F is reached (as these are already cooked, and are reheating 165F is not required).

Food Cost Considerations

Once again, there are many books and resources when discussing restaurant finances and determining your food cost. The example that I used is here: (http://www.wikihow.com/Calculate-Food-Cost). I will not make a big point of this but just highlight a few things specific to BBQ, and will not go into individual menu items as there are to many variables such as pricing differences in individual markets and your choice of menu items.

I do need to point out a few things specific to BBQ restaurants and that's the seasonal food cost fluctuations and shrinkage/waste when doing your costing...As most of your meat choices are likely tied to the Futures Market (world wide Market trading) you will get seasonal variations (sometimes massive) in pricing. When the Asian markets start buying pork in quantities our prices go up! You want to get the highest price per pound for the last 12 months (your meat vendor should be able to supply you with this) and use the highest cost for menu pricing.

We do need to consider shrinkage and waste. As food cooks it shrinks and you must account for this variable, Brisket (nose/deckel on) may require some trimming and is also waste.

ItemLoss from Cooking/Trim

Pork 40%

Brisket 45%

Chicken 30%

Management and POS (Point of Sale) Systems Explained

When we opened our first restaurant we took orders by hand which was troublesome at times. Even bad handwriting which led to incomplete or inaccurate orders was not the primary issue. It was tracking sales and knowing where we stood financially, what was selling and what should be removed from the menu altogether.

> Beware – salesmen will come into your establishment and try to sell you on a free POS if you sign up for their credit card processing. Give these offers great scrutiny, as they may have additional charges or higher rates for transactions that you may not have to pay with another vendor. In the long run, you could pay more than twice or higher for that free POS.

We looked at dozens of Point of Sale (POS) Systems. Most were very good but very expensive. In addition to the hardware cost, a few required "maintenance agreements" for upgrades and technical support. I was in IT for over 20 years. I think I know what I'm doing...

I won't bore you with all the great stuff a computerized POS can do. That's what Google is for. I'll just go ahead and tell you which one we chose, and why, but feel free to hunt the market, there may be one you like better!

As I am an experienced IT guy, I chose to acquire my own hardware (well, from my basement anyway) and ordered a few things I did not have (like CC redears) from amazon.com.

If you do not feel confident in this, or just don't want to deal with any maintnance issues that arise, there are plenty of "turn-key" offers available as well.

But, I will make an effort to explain te components that make up a system so you are better educated when shopping.

You will see some differences in the hardware you find online and what I have. Many are "all-in-ones", which means the entire computer is housed in the monitor screen, and not separate components. Other than that, there is little difference.

The system we went with is called **PointOS**

Highlights

For all it's capabilities it's cheap at $99 per year per license

No "maintenance agreement", and tech support is free

Upgrades are free

Partnered with Merchant Warehouse (credit card processor) so taking credit cards is a snap

Instant knowledge of the days sales (day, week, month, and year(s)

I ran PointOS on 2 older Windows XP machines with 512mb ram, keyboard and mice I had in my basement. The programs hardware requirements are minimal and saw no need for Windows 8, 10, etc or newer hardware. But this is your choice. I'm just cheap.

Additional hardware I do recommend

15" LCD monitor, no more
(don't want to be peeking over it to see your customer)
<u>note</u>: I did try touch screens, but they're not the most durable, and broke often.

Epson TM-T88 (III, or IV) Thermal Receipt Printers with Parallel or USB interface *(more on these printers and setup in a moment)*

Epson Printer compatible Cash Drawer *(more on this too)*

Laser Printer *(optional but helpful for printing takeout menu's and reports)*

USB Credit Card Readers *(get 2, they are cheap and need a backup)*

When looking for receipt printers there are WAY too many options, and interfaces which can get confusing and may cost you money if you're not careful and end up with the wrong device.

For the setup I use, you need a computer with either a Parallel Printer Port (used for older printer connectivity), and or plenty (5 or more) USB interfaces.

Having a Parallel Port just gives you another option when shopping for a receipt printer. The USB models can be expensive, and they still produce the parallel versions of these printers so having another connection option for multiple printer styles is better.

Why an Epson printer? They are the most common and pretty much set the standard for receipt printer Hex Addressed Signals used for printer function, and other serial devices that may connect to the printer directly such as the cash drawer.

Use Caution When Shopping for a Receipt Printer

There are a number of Serial Connectivity options when it comes to these printers. Stay away from anything with a RS-232 Serial *(looks like a phone cable connection),* descriptions that say Parallel/Serial *(requiring an adapter, so not parallel)* or a direct 9 pin Serial Interface. Unless you already have this type of cabling in a location you are considering and can VERIFY that it is functional, otherwise avoid it. Stick to the plan.

This is a Parallel Printer Interface *(just in case you are too young to remember)*

OR a USB Interface is acceptable.

Setting Up Your POS

Setup your computer as normal, and have Windows installed.

Download and install PointOS 30 Day trial.

You do not need to have a Receipt Printer or Cash Drawer setup/installed in order to use this program. I do recommend you start by reading the Manger Manual and user Manuals to familiarize yourself with the product.

If you should have a question on the program their Tech Support Team is very helpful, and you get full support even with the trial version!

Printer and Cash Drawer Setup

You must first get the printer setup. Unlike most printer setups (using the "Add Printer Wizard" in Windows you must download the driver/setup software from Epson https://pos.epson.com/developers/techresdetails.htm?ProductPK=642

Once you have the driver setup and the printer is working (do a test print) you can then setup the cash drawer. This is the easy part. There is a serial cable coming out the back of the drawer. Looks just like a phone plug. This is a serial cable. It plugs into the identical port on the back of the printer.

So, when you ring up a sale it will then print the receipt for the customer which will then "kick" the cash drawer open. That's it.

Once you have a few menu items programmed into PointOS try doing a few test sales and smile as the drawer flies open! I did!

Here are a few screen shots of our setup.

Order Entry Screen

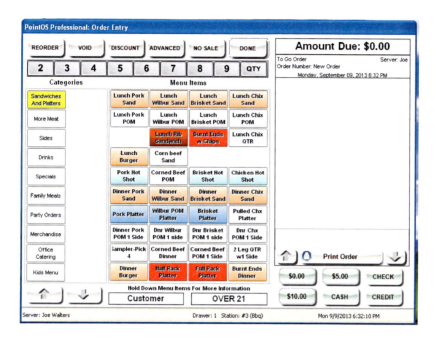

One of my favorite features was the Delivery screen with built in Google Map Access!

Taking Credit Cards

I have been to plenty of BBQ restaurants that did not take cards, but in every case they where in more rural areas, or local to the neighborhood. We really resisted as long as we could just to avoid that hassle. But if you want the catering business you need to take cards. In the few months that we were open, before having a POS or taking cards I know I lost at least $5000 in business.

Another reason I like taking them is guaranteed funds. If a company pays with a check how do you know it's good? I know, there are fees involved, but you can "build them" into your pricing and on large orders you will be able to cover it regardless.

Taking Cards Is Easy

If you use are using PointOS its as easy as calling Merchant Warehouse http://merchantwarehouse.com/ and requesting a new Merchant Application. As they are an affiliate company, it made things a lot easier. Regardless of which system you go with the steps of getting an account should be the same.

They will setup an electronic application for you to sign digitally within 24 hours. Have all your company information (tax ID, address, banking information, etc).

It will take another 48-72 hours for them to verify you, and your company and get approval from an underwriter (for security reasons mainly as fraud in the industry is prevalent).

Once they have verified you are a real company, they will want to schedule a test of the account. If the test is successful you are done!

If you are concerned about your credit being a problem, don't be. The checks they perform are mainly about fraud prevention and being unemployed for a year I had more than a few "dings", and never had a problem.

The Not So Glamorous - Cleaning

Cleaning Schedules Are Vital

When you cook BBQ you can be sure of one thing and that's a mess. Grease, dry rub, raw meat, the smoker with grease all up in it, all of it. It's just plain messy.

The best way to save time and labor (money) is to have a daily schedule rather than a long weekend night or a entire Sunday to do it. There are usually slow periods each day to get these tasks completed *(between lunch and dinner for example)*. These are "deep cleans". Pull it out from the wall and really get your head in it kinda clean!

Here Is Our Schedule:

Monday – Warmer Drawers and Steam Table

Tuesday - Hot Holding Cabinets (I had three)

Wednesday – Coolers

Thursday – Ovens

Friday – Too busy to deep clean

Saturday – Too busy to deep clean

Sunday – Smoker

We were closed on Sunday's, perfect time to get it done as there was no production.

Cleaning the Smoker

Cleaning the smoker was imperative to avoid grease fires that can and did occur. The weekly cleaning was just removing the shelves scraping them down, drained out the grease, and emptied the firebox. A deep clean consisted of the above but we went one step further:

1. First we called the Fire Department and let them know what we were doing *(they would sometimes come out to watch)*.

2. We broke up a pallet and threw all the wood inside the smoking chamber *(where you put the meat)*.

3. Threw a little bit of the grease from the smoker on the wood and light it up!

   It's like putting your oven on the Clean Setting but on a much larger scale! With Flames! It was always a sight to behold. We had a Fire Extinguisher but I doubt it would have helped anything. To snuff out a fire like this if you should ever encounter one accidentally is simply cut off the oxygen. Closing the lid always did the trick.

DO NOT use water on a smoker fire! Ever!

That Nasty Grease Trap Next to the Sink

The function of the grease trap is pretty apparent. It catches most of the nasty stuff when washing pans, and I mean nasty. You will need to have this thing cleaned out, about every 4-6 months. It consists of a pumper truck coming out and sucking that stuff out. It takes about 20 minutes and cost about $100-125 per service. Do it in the morning before you open.

The smell is pretty bad and you don't want your customers to think its you.

I also wanted to point out one more time that when you buy a 3 compartment sink that your grease trap MUST be of adequate size for the sink volume and its flow.

If you don't know what size trap you need (I would call to verify) call your Health or Building department. They will ask you for the measurements of one of the sink bowls (width, height, and depth). They will then tell you how many gallons of trap capacity you will need for it.

Trust me, when a trap cost $500, you want to get the right one before you install it and find out its not.

Plumbing Lines Cleaned

The amount of grease that a BBQ joint produces is amazing. This will sometimes "gum up" the pipes, and you will need to get your lines cleaned (snaked) about twice a year. At least we did.

So you will want to find a good local plumber and come to terms. If he knows he has guaranteed work twice a year, and is paid cash, most will give you a good break. When I say local I mean small (independent) plumber. The larger guys don't really make deals. They are to busy anyway and a small job isn't worth it.

Ice Machine

These need to be cleaned at least every 6 months. They can get mold and algae in the slats that the ice forms in and sediment/hard water will block the water passages. Ice machines are very temperamental and require a lot of maintenance compared to other kitchen equipment.

That's why I preferred to "rent" my ice machine. I used a company call Easy Ice http://www.easyice.com/ . For about $130 per month I got an ice machine installed.

What did the "rent cover?

Scheduled cleanings

Repairs (if you have hard water, the tubes clog often)

Reimbursed us for any ice we had to buy when it was down

No contract

And the best part is the upfront savings. Even a small ice machine cost $3000, and the point of this book is to get you open with as little money as possible, so $130 to get ice is a bargain.

What to Expect Opening Day

This is where I need to set realistic expectation form the start.

Most restaurants (even great ones) have built their business on two things, great food and *Word of Mouth*. It takes time for word to spread that you are open, and have awesome BBQ!

In the first few weeks you will wonder what happened. You did everything right, but where are the crowds? Relax! This is just part of the process. Don't get upset and take it personally!

Then it will be like a light switch. It will just "turn on". We always had a busy lunch as that was how we started, serving lunch outside. But understand, you (we) are dealing with 2 sets of customers. Those that worked in the town during the day but lived somewhere else (lunch crowd), and those that work somewhere else but live in town (dinner crowd).. We started with only a few customers for dinner one day and a line out the door another. Be patient.

Don't make 500lbs of pork, and 100 racks of ribs!

The cool thing we did that's perfectly acceptable in a BBQ joint was having a white-board at the counter that displaying the meats and side dishes that were ready to be served.

It became a challenge to our customers to score some ribs or brisket before they ran out! It gave them a sense of accomplishment when they saw them on the board. This was great to watch until we got a consistent flow and could determine our volume better. It also prevented waste.

Staffing

If everything goes as planned you WILL need help. Now I'm not going to bore you with a bunch of laws and HR stuff that you'll find in other books, and online. I'm just going to present you with some realities of the restaurant world. Sometimes it's not pretty, and can be down right frustrating.

I'm trying not to be particularly derogatory about restaurant workers, but there is a reason why someone will work as hard as a kitchen worker does for that small amount of pay. What I'm pointing out is that reason may be something you may or may not want to know about. There are many stories back in the kitchen about their past as well as their present.

The good ones will work like a dog for the low pay because they are building themselves back up, or just wanting to pay their way through school and "a-job-is-a-job". I really appreciate the hard work that many of my staff did.

Others caused a lot of frustration. The average length of stay for a restaurant worker is around 6 months. The good ones keep stepping up and the bad ones are filtered out. It's just the way it is.

Some of those work hard to turn their lives around, but suffer from the complications they are living with from the past. More times than I care about, this bled into my workplace, be it from their attendance, attitude, crazy girlfriends, baby-mommas, people they owe money to, you name it.

What we found in our area is that alcohol and drug use were common with these types of workers, so you have to keep a close eye on things. Some have a strong enough work ethic to keep work and outside life separated, while others aren't as ethical. If someone says they are in remission or have conquered a habit, ask how long it's been. We've had a couple fall off the wagon during work and it made for a very stressful situation, but we feel everyone (with a few exceptions) deserves a chance.

Believe it or not, some of our best employees were teenagers. Our son, Devoreaux was a great judge of character between his school chums. He looked beyond the ones he'd like to hang out with and invited them to apply only if he thought they'd actually work...probably because he knew he'd hear it from us, otherwise. All of the kids he recommended had great attendance and worked well together, which is the best thing you can ask for from an employee. Most of them worked for us through their high school years, too.

A couple of the teens were great at the many kitchen duties, and some were great at the front of the house. We had them until the next transition in their lives (school, summer vacations, college). Our son and his best friend, Chad even managed to be great pit-masters as they progressed through the years. When they were Seniors in High School, we could trust either of them to run any part of the store with confidence, and we could step away and trust them to it. Now that they're in college, they may never turn back, and working in a restaurant did teach them the value of a good education!

At the beginning, you're going to be there at all time, so you can keep things under control. You've got to walk away once in a while, so you'll need someone you can trust to keep things going while you are away, be it for a trip for supplies, illness, or a family trip to your in-laws when you feel really confident!

At first, my pinch-hitter was my wife, and she worked as hard as I did. I cannot tell you how many managers I've gone through though. Promoting someone to manager was like sprinkling pixie dust on them and they thought that their new job was to boss people around instead of lift a finger and they became an instant jerk. Finding someone with real management training was going to be expensive.

I worked the smoker at first and had a kitchen helper. My wife ran the front of the house. Between lunch and dinner, she would run and get supplies while I ran the front and could step back and forth to the smoker as needed. As she transitioned out, I was fortunate enough to get a couple people with a high enough multi-tasking aptitude to pit-master as well as handle the other kitchen tasks. This skill is not the common norm, so you will work through a few (or many) people to find that perfect combination.

The same goes for the front of the house. I don't think anyone was as congenial and engaging to our customers as my wife and I were. We loved how running our place transitioned us from being "residents" to "members" of our community. This showed in how we acted with the customers.

We had a few who were 'pretty good' up front, and one who worked so well with my wife, that when they worked together, the customers dubbed it "The Val and Stacy Show". They had a lot of fun together, and it was contagious across the whole dining room. Once again – "6 month rule, and everyone has a story". I'm sure some robbed us blind too, so as the owner, keep your hands on the money yourself.

So all this being said – take the time when you're interviewing them to get down to their psyche and listen to your gut. If I liked someone I interviewed, I would invite them for an "audition", and it could be at that very moment. I wanted to observe how they worked and see how fast they caught on. I could get an idea after a day or two if they could handle all that was required. If they passed, they were offered the job. If not, I paid them for their time and wished them luck elsewhere.

If you find good people that are not overqualified and likely to move on within the 6 month rule, do all you can to keep them happy with you. Show your appreciation genuinely, and it doesn't have to cost anything. A little praise like a high-five for a job well done can go a long way so don't forget to do it.

Payroll and Other Stuff

There are a few options out there for handling this kind of stuff. Most depends on the level of effort and time you have, and how much you're willing to spend to NOT do it. Quickbooks is a common and fairly easy accounting software to learn and use. It has its own payroll section and can figure out your taxes and such. Just don't forget to send the checks for everyone's state, local, federal, unemployment taxes and child support payments. Yeah, all of that.

A couple of alternatives is outsourcing these tasks out:

You can go to the lighter point of a payroll company who gets the total hours worked on Monday, tells you Tuesday how much money you need in the bank to cover the checks, then can either direct-deposits everyone's pay or send you hard-copy checks. They charge a reasonable fee for every pay period and take over all that paperwork. You may have a local person who does this kind of stuff on the side, too, so ask around.

Another alternative is HR-partner companies who basically hire your employees and outsource them back to you. The fees are still reasonable, but they take care of the workers comp insurance and everything. They keep everything on the up-and-up.

Final Thoughts

Bear with me here – it's my final brain dump, and not necessarily in any order:

If you are doing the mobile thing first consider yourself hardcore. I really enjoyed staying up all night getting the pork and other items ready. I loved the smell of the evening air. No one around, and plenty of time to plan my businesses next move. Searching the internet for great equipment deals, looking for a good restaurant location and figuring out my money strategy to make the plan come together. I must say that the days were long, but they were the best times I had. Felt empowering. It was all up to us. There were times I wish I was still at that stage.

But if you want to build it into something great, have a plan. Everything is in the plan. I don't mean a business plan either. I feel that those are TOO structured in the early stages. Be "fluid, but focused" in your approach. Look for opportunities all the time to grow the business and make money. Don't be a pest, but be opportunistic. Don't settle. If something you consider to be pretty *close (price, opportunity for a location, party or event, whatever),* but does not fit with your desired business model skip it. Move on. There are tons of them out there that are "close". Stick to the plan, and look for those things that do fit. Make them mold to your requirements if possible to make them work (*fluid, with focus…*). But don't bend. If you do, you will do it more and you will lose focus.

Opening any business, especially one as competitive as a restaurant, can be daunting. Yeah, doing what you love does make going to work a little brighter, but it's still a business. Treat it like one; it's not a hobby anymore.

To that end, I recommend your first restaurant be of sufficient size that you can manage *(and obviously afford).* Start small and develop your customer base and the processes that work for you. GROW the business. Too big too fast and you risk too much too soon.

If you sign a lease and find you are growing out of the space and need to move, you are still responsible to pay the rent until someone else comes in. So, take that into consideration while looking for your first restaurant. A smaller space in a really good retail area will mitigate a lot of this as the space will not stay empty long.

Be creative in your approach to things. Look at new ways of doing things, and improving the food, and the business. I did, you are reading my creativeness right now. Every technique in this book was once just an idea I had - tried it, and improved along the way. Improve on these ideas yourself. Yeah, learning these techniques will cut years off the "trial-&-error" method but don't stop there. If you start with these processes, imagine where you will be 3-4 years from now!

Do not waiver from your expectations of what should be done and how. If not, others (staff) will make that decision for you and you will be working more than you need.

Vendors and other individuals will constantly be calling, wanting to speak with you about something "urgent", or just walk in and expect you to talk, and always right before opening! Inconsiderate bastards! TELL THEM NO. Let them know it's not cool to call or stop in during service!

Don't take excuses and crap from the staff either. If something is made wrong, show them how to do it right. If they do it wrong again, feel free to show them you're not "happy". If they do it wrong again, and the situation calls for it (ruining a Brisket) send them home for a few days. Trust me; they will get it right the next time. If not, fire them...Period. I had to learn to let people go, I still hate it, but it's just business.

You spend a lot of time getting someone trained and putting out a good product. You don't need one staff member screwing it up. Also, if the other staff sees this going on and not getting resolved they too will become lazy, or even pissed if they are doing a good job and one person is getting away with screwing up. Good kitchen staff takes pride in their work!

Do your best to get supplies in the morning or right after you close, if possible. Something always comes up and you need to take the time to get it done before it does.

If you have the kitchen staff prepare the shopping list, double check it yourself. I can't tell you how many times they had me either buy or order things you don't need because they didn't see it on the shelf (or didn't look), or missed something altogether requiring another trip that was needed. This business is about Cash Flow and time, and too much inventory is bad. Set reasonable par levels and make sure they understand the business and how over-ordering affects it.

Be patient, especially with the customers. You will hear things from them that may make you want to bust out laughing *(they see pink and thinks it's not cooked, but don't know a smoke ring when they see it)* or upsetting. Listen and acknowledge the problem. This is not kissing ass, its opportunity to do things better. Whether it educating the customer, or finding they are correct and there is a problem, either way you want to hear about it!

Suggest you watch EVERY episode of Ramsey's Kitchen Nightmare's at least once. I watched them three times (plenty of late nights smoking…). Do not be one of those foolish, intolerant, self-obsessed restaurant owners that DOES NOTHING WRONG. Your food is not perfect all the time, as that's not possible. Be willing to listen to complaints and or the situation, and learn from it!
The sooner you learn to not take it personally the faster you can react to these situations.

Also, watch the moving "Waiting…", as it's a comedy all about what shenanigans go on behind the scenes at a restaurant. Did I mention that you don't want ANY of these things to occur at your own place. You'll love it and cringe at the same time.

Well, all I can say is thank you for reading this. I hope it answered many of your questions and gave you a sound starting point.

Thanks again and GOOD LUCK!

The End...

Made in the USA
San Bernardino, CA
22 January 2019